BOATHOUSE TREASURE

William D. Van Atta Jr.

Dedication

To my mom, dad, three brothers and three sisters, for all their loving support over the years. To the many precious furry and winged companions, I have had the honor of experiencing life with.

Acknowledgement

I would like to give special thanks to my mom, who introduced me to the poems of her grandfather, Joseph Russell Taylor, and his acquaintance, Robert W. Service. Thank you to the many teachers who patiently helped me with my deficient reading and writing skills.

For introducing me to the North Woods, I would like to thank the Whiteways—Dr. Robert (Red) and his wife, Marion. I worked my way through college as the Whiteways' handyman.

About the Author

William (Bill) D. Van Atta Jr. is a veteran Army aviator and retired registered nurse who is a native of the Midwest, now living in La Crescent, Minnesota. Bill holds a Bachelor of Science degree in geography from the University of Wisconsin–La Crosse.

After 12 years of service in the U.S. Army as both a rotary-wing and fixed-wing aviator, Bill went back to school. He graduated from The Norfolk General Hospital School of Nursing and then completed his Bachelor of Science in Nursing degree at Excelsior University and was licensed as an RN.

Bill practiced in several hospitals, including Level 1 and Level 2 trauma centers, where he specialized in the care of surgical, trauma, and burn patients.

When not writing, Bill enjoys spending time with his dogs. He especially likes being outdoors—camping, hiking, and photographing nature. Over the past couple of years, Bill has been putting his woodworking skills to the test building a small sailboat. He is an avid swimmer and has competed in several open water swimming competitions.

You can connect with Bill at: running_wolf57@yahoo.com

Isn't it funny how the whisper of a word, a smell carried on the wind, the sound of an old familiar song, or simply a quick glance and touch of a cherished item can take you back to the past? I was cleaning my bedroom this morning when this happened, and I was taken back—back to a time long ago on a lake in Canada and the boathouse treasure.

All packed up, we settled into the baby blue VW Squareback and left La Crosse behind. It was late afternoon, and so began the eight-hour drive to Nestor Falls, Ontario, Canada. Behind the wheel to start the trip was Dr. Whiteway, also known as Red. Then there was me, riding shotgun. I was a college student working as the Whiteways' hired hand. Taking up the backseat was Nicholas, the Russian Wolfhound.

Driving nonstop through the late spring night, we travelled north, skirting the mighty Mississippi along the Great River Road towards the Twin Cities. We listened to Minnesota Public Radio as long as we could, and when we lost the signal, we tuned the dial to whatever we could find.

We made good time with Dr. Whiteway's lead foot, him ignoring the yellow and black placard placed on the dash by one of his kids. It read in bold black letters: "Slow Down."

As it got dark, Nick and I fell asleep. When I woke up, the Twin Cities were far behind, and we were in northern Minnesota nearing the Canadian border. The night sky was taking on the pinkish glow of morning. More and more lakes started to fill the landscape, and a scent of pine lingered in the air.

We arrived at International Falls, stopped for gas and a few dry goods, then meandered our way through town to the border crossing. Our time to get through Canadian customs was brief. Just a few questions, a quick inspection, and a friendly pat on Nick's head, and we were official. We passed the "Welcome to Canada" sign and moved on.

Now clear of the border and Fort Frances, we started to get excited, for the lake was but an hour away. This last hour of the drive always seemed to be the longest. We continued north, Lake of the Woods not far off to the west and Rainy Lake to the east. Nick poked his head out the window, taking in the new smells. He wagged his tail with approval.

We weaved through the forest, past a seaplane base, then took a right turn onto the gravel road that opened to Kakagi Lake and Hanson's Hideaway Lodge.

I was always awestruck as Kakagi's magical beauty was revealed before my eyes: the deep blue waters, rocky shoreline, magnificent forests, and the puffy white clouds. We unloaded our gear, then started our walk to the camp store. Looking back at the dock, we could see the boat was already in the water waiting for us.

Entering the store, we found Ken Hanson stocking some goods. Ken and Dr. Whiteway greeted each other, then struck up a conversation. As they talked, I looked around the store, eyeing some things I could take home and give as gifts. I overheard Dr. Whiteway ask Ken if the lake water was still safe to drink, and Ken replied that it was.

We gathered up a few items: fresh bread, some preserves, a slab of uncut bacon, and some fresh linens for the lodge. Saying goodbye to Ken, we headed for the boat.

We quickly loaded up, started the boat's twin Evinrude outboards, and with Dr. Whiteway at the helm, headed eastward to the far side of the lake. The lake was tame this morning, making for a dry, comfortable ride.

As we glided across the water, I reminisced about the previous year at the lake. That summer, we fell several pines, stripped their bark, and set them up for drying. One of the guests that year was the son of one of the Whiteways' friends in Chicago.

When we had free time, he'd take the aluminum skiff out, terrorizing the quiet waters while racing about the bays, blaring Neil Diamond songs from his boombox. I enjoy a Neil Diamond tune but not in the Canadian wilderness. Here, I enjoy the many sounds and songs you hear when tuned to nature. To this day, "Cracklin' Rosie" takes me back to those days.

This year, there was no boy from Chicago, no boombox, no Neil Diamond.

Dr. Whiteway navigated the boat through the waters, passing by several islands and avoiding the shallows that lay hidden beneath the lake. We rounded one last island, and the dock at the Whiteways' Kakagi Lodge, with its welcoming Canadian flag, came into view. The boat slowed, and we drifted to the dock.

The lodge, built in the 1930s, was resurrected from years of abandonment and now, with its subdued green siding, sat proudly looking west across the lake. A couple of families shared the lodge. It was now Dr. Whiteway's turn to enjoy some time there.

The great room, a focal point of the dwelling, had a large stone fireplace with a huge bull moose head above it. In the afternoon, the moose was illuminated as light shone through the west-facing dormer across from it. There was a large screened porch off the great room where you could watch the beautiful sunsets while gently swinging on the porch swing.

There was no running water, no electricity, and no generator. Water was brought to the lodge from the lake in galvanized steel pails. Bathing was done in the lake. The kitchen did have a propane-fueled stove and refrigerator.

This would be my second time at the lake helping the Whiteways with the construction of their personal log cabin on the grounds. This year, we were starting on the construction of the foundation and subflooring. We were the first to arrive at the lodge, so we had to open things up and prepare it for the season. This included removing locks, stocking the refrigerator and pantry, hooking up the propane for the stove and refrigerator, and lastly picking the rooms we would sleep in, then unpacking and making beds.

By the time we finished, most of the day was gone. We cooked up a quick dinner, then sat on the porch to watch the sunset. We were all quite tired. We lit the lanterns as it became dark, then headed for our rooms. Tomorrow we would resume the construction of the new cabin.

The dawn broke, the loons started laughing, and rays of soft light filtered through the cobweb-decorated windows. I could hear tiny feet outside walking across the roof—maybe squirrels or crows? Wiping the sleep from my eyes, I rolled out of my warm bed and met the chilly morning air. As I got dressed, I could smell breakfast cooking. I followed my nose up to the kitchen where I enjoyed some eggs, bacon, and toast with Dr. Whiteway and Nick.

After cleaning up from breakfast, we headed outside to inspect the logs we cut the previous year. All the logs looked good.

We then proceeded to the building site. The planned site had a northwestern view of the water on a rock outcropping that sloped toward the shoreline.

We worked clearing loose debris from the cabin footprint, marked out the footing locations, and then took a break for lunch and an afternoon bath and swim.

I put on my swimsuit and gathered up some soap. We used Ivory soap because it floats. I also picked up a towel and shampoo—yes, I had hair back then.

Taking a bath in frigid Kakagi was a simple task once you got the nerve to jump in. To start, you took the jump, then quickly climbed out, lathered up, and jumped back in for the rinse. If you were brave, you would swim around for a while, then climb out as you were getting numb or when visions of Sam McGee and the "Alice May" appeared.[1]

On some days, after working up a sweat, I would climb the ladder to the boathouse roof and take the ten-foot plunge to the waters below. It was from the roof the previous year that I first saw the old sunken boat on the lake bottom a few yards from the boathouse entrance. I believe it was a Chris-Craft runabout with an inboard engine.

The story told was that years ago it caught fire, burned to the waterline, and sank. There were some black-and-white photos of the boat during its early days on the lake.

---

[1] Sam McGee and the "Alice May", are mentioned in the poem, The Cremation of Sam McGee, by Robert W. Service

They hung on the wall in the lodge with other pictures from the past. This year, I brought my dive mask, fins, and snorkel and planned to take a closer look at the wreck.

Now all dried off, warmed up, and dressed, I went back up the path to the lodge for some relaxation and a snack.

Working at the lodge was generally easygoing. We worked every day but always took time to relax and enjoy the beautiful surroundings.

The next task at the building site was to build up the foundation on the rocky ground. This involved drilling rebar into the rock and constructing concrete piers. We had to make our own concrete, which meant taking a trip to Sand Island. We chose a nice day for the trip to the island. We loaded the boat with some large buckets, a shovel, and a screen for cleaning debris from the sand. Climbing aboard, we shoved off the dock and headed north to find the island's hidden sandy beach.

After a 20-minute ride, we found the island and beached the boat. There was a coarse grinding sound as the boat rubbed against the sandy bottom. We climbed over the side and helped Nick out of the boat. While he sniffed around, we got organized to collect the sand we would use for the concrete mix. Shoveling away, we scooped up the coarse sand, sifting it through the screen into the buckets. We continued scooping and sifting for an hour or two as Nick supervised from the tree line.

Once we had enough sand, we all climbed back in the boat, fired up the motors, and headed back to the lodge.

We continued our work on the cabin, and it was coming along nicely. We drilled the rock and built up piers that the floor support beams would rest on.

Some days I would spend my free time canoeing about the lake. One day I headed out in the early evening so I could take some sunset pictures. On my way, I stopped at the island just west of the lodge and dumped a collection of compost on a rock near the water's edge. The crows would congregate on the rock and noisily eat up whatever goodies they could find.

Kakagi in Ojibway is translated as black bird, so the lake also became known as Crow Lake.

I got back to paddling again and found a good spot to take some shots of the sunset. I set my tripod up in some shallow water, mounted the camera, and waited for the magic.

The sunset was starting to take place. I began shooting. The shutter clicked away as the sun began its descent toward the horizon. The colors started out a pale yellow, then progressed to pink, orange, and finally a fiery red that was reflected in the still waters. The colors faded, and darkness was not far behind.

I gathered up my gear, climbed back into the canoe, and started the race back to the boathouse. It was a race for sure—a race against the gathering swarm of hungry mosquitoes. I paddled faster and faster, and the black cloud chasing me grew larger and darker.

I managed to beat them to the boathouse but lost time tying up the canoe. Without warning, the bloodsuckers were upon my skin, and I started my sprint to the safe haven of the lodge. There, I took shelter behind the slamming screen door.

To avoid night bites from any stray mosquitoes that made it inside, we would shut the windows and doors and spray insecticide throughout the bedrooms. Looking back, this was probably not a good idea. At least we got to sleep peacefully.

The long Canadian days seemed to pass by too quickly, and my time at Kakagi would soon be over. Still, I hadn't gotten a close look at the sunken boat. One afternoon, after nailing some floor joists, I suited up, grabbed my snorkeling gear, and headed down to the boathouse for some wreck diving.

The water was a little warmer than a few weeks ago, but it was still cold. I had a neoprene vest that helped somewhat with the cool water. I donned my gear and jumped in. I swam out, soon found the boat, and started my dive to the bottom to check it out. The wreck was in about ten feet of water.

Holding my breath for as long as I could, I surveyed it from stern to bow. I came up for air, then went down again. I was hoping to find some souvenirs or salvageable items. There wasn't much left of the craft except for the engine and some of the boat's hull. I took one last breath and swam down. This time, I went to the stern and looked underneath. I found the rudder and a large brass propeller half buried in the mud. I surfaced, caught my breath, and decided to call it a day.

That night, lying in bed, I thought about the brass propeller and came up with a plan.

In the morning, over breakfast, I told Dr. Whiteway about my dive on the old boat and my idea—my plan to remove the propeller from the wreck. He listened intently and gave his approval. That afternoon, after work, I began my salvage operation.

This time, wrench in hand, I dove to the bottom of the boat. It took several dives to adjust the wrench to fit the nut that secured the propeller. With a final adjustment, I dove to the propeller, placed the wrench on the nut, and pulled with all my strength. The nut didn't budge. I made several dives to try to remove the nut with no luck. It was time for another plan.

I decided that the only option was to cut the propeller free, but that would have to wait until tomorrow. I updated Dr. Whiteway, and he was able to locate a hacksaw among several tools in the utility room.

That afternoon, I returned to the wreck and, saw in hand, started cutting away the nut. Dive after dive, I held my breath, sawing away at the nut until it finally fell away. I returned to the surface and rested for a while.

I caught my breath, then returned to the bottom to remove the prop from the shaft. I pulled and pulled, but the old boat refused to give up its propeller. I even tried pounding it free with no luck. It was then that I decided to cut the drive shaft where it exited the hull.

Obsessed and determined, I returned to the bottom again and again until the saw blade made it through the inch-and-a-half-thick steel shaft. I floated to the surface, exhausted, and rested on my back. I made one last dive to the bottom to grab the propeller and shaft and bring it to the surface.

Cradling it in my arms, I swam with it to the boathouse dock and removed it from the water. As I climbed onto the dock, Dr. Whiteway came down the path. We both grinned as we closely inspected the treasure.

My days at Kakagi were coming to an end. We were able to finish up the subfloor on the cabin and place a couple of logs, and then it was time to listen to the crying loons while watching one last sunset.

In the morning, we would turn the lodge over to another family, then return south.

I dusted off the old propeller and placed it back in a corner of my bedroom. Seeing it and touching it had taken me back to the lake, to the boathouse, and to the sunken treasure I found there many years ago.

It was then that I came to realize that the treasure wasn't the old boat's propeller at all, but the many cherished memories I had of my days in the Canadian wilderness on a lake named Kakagi.

Prologue

I never got to see the completed cabin. My life, careers, and new adventures consumed my time. Still, I think of my days in Canada and see a trip north in the future.

The reference to "Sam McGee" and the "Alice May" in the story is from a poem written by Robert W. Service, The Cremation of Sam McGee. It is one of my favorites.

KAKAGI LODGE
NESTOR FALLS
ONTARIO

www.ingramcontent.com/pod-product-compliance
Lightning Source LLC
Chambersburg PA
CBHW041134120626

46547CB00019B/2985